VOLUNTARY

Adam Thorpe

CAPE POETRY

Published by Jonathan Cape 2012

2 4 6 8 10 9 7 5 3 1

First published in Great Britain in 2012 by
Jonathan Cape
Random House, 20 Vauxhall Bridge Road,
London SW1V 2SA

www.randomhouse.co.uk

Addresses for companies within The Random House Group Limited can be found at:
www.randomhouse.co.uk/offices.htm

The Random House Group Limited Reg. No. 954009

A CIP catalogue record for this book
is available from the British Library

ISBN 9780224094177

The Random House Group Limited supports The Forest Stewardship Council (FSC®), the
leading international forest certification organisation. Our books carrying the FSC label are
printed on FSC® certified paper. FSC is the only forest certification scheme endorsed by
the leading environmental organisations, including Greenpeace. Our paper procurement
policy can be found at www.randomhouse.co.uk/environment

in memory of
John Fairfax

CONTENTS

IMPRESSION

The pawprint, bedded on the Roman tile
our late neighbour bequeathed us,

is deep enough, even on a roof's pitch,
to pool rain as petals do

or to take a cast from, revive
the rough pads that time would have tossed away

if the dog had never trotted across
those flat, glistening squares of clay

laid to dry on the sun-bright turf
at the back of the works . . .

or hopped rather, for the paw's impress
is unaccompanied, its claw-dots risen

at the sides like fork pricks in dough.
I like the back of the *tegula*, too, those arrested

shadows of grass and grit: the earth's muddle
just as it was, two thousand years ago —

the shabby mongrel, lamish, yelled at;
the jobsworth muttering as he crouches down,

It'll still keep the rain off. It'll do.

SUTTON HOO

The Overflow Car Park's empty,
the light a lustrous grey on birch.

The local farmer's cut his turf
right to the ligeance, so it's just this corner,

discreetly fenced in wire. A spellbound
darkness of firs at the field's edge.

Several shaggy swells: which one?
With history's mood-swings it's hard

to tell. There's gold for some, though;
while my sense of nation's less a buried crown

than a stain of post-hole, or this viewing
rostrum I try to work things out from.

HOME VIDEOS

We run them all through in a glut
on the veteran machine, wincing and laughing
at what never resembles who we think we are
or thought we were, for everything is chafing
not to remain, not to get caught in the rut
we'd quite like to stay in, now we are here.

And everyone is still alive;
it's all a lie, death is. The shock of the young,
although we did not feel young then. Our wonder
that the boys could ever not have been strong
men accompanies our surprise at their five-
year-old sister sticking her tongue out, stealing their thunder

over ten years off from where we are,
like a nearby star. Explorers of the Amazon
in a garden we hardly recognise (their *cabane*
of sticks and fruit crates long in oblivion),
these children were definitely ours, turn and stare
and make faces, as if we're the ones that should run

away in pretend fright,
seeing how fast the passing birthdays go,
so resembling each other – the off-camera burst
at a joke that has vanished forever, the slow
lighting of the candles that refuse to light,
the pinned donkey's tail in focus at last.

It keeps the detail, unlike
memory. Whole swathes obliterated in between
cannot be loaded and screened, we know. This
is the only stake that's held, and time is mean,
and it always stops mid-show, like a lightning strike
followed by a blizzard – and this triumphant hiss.

SIGHTING

Of course we were always meant
to watch its slicked-down head

appear and reappear in the Sound's
rocky inlet beyond the lane's

verge at dusk; but whether
it feeds or plays or is simply

luxuriating in the violet
gloom and glitter of the sea

after its den's blind room
we have no idea, knowing

next to nothing about any creature.
It vanishes only to be

repeatedly spotted – allotted
half-an-hour of our lives

before the excitement palls
and the binoculars are left

on the sill, no longer fought for. What
doesn't, in the end, become familiar

all round, however strange or fine?
I wish that sea-otter's amazement was mine.

FUEL

She has to store five tons
to see through winter. I offer
her a hand, but she waves her own.

She's carrying just a few a day
from where they were delivered
to the shed: twenty yards. It's early May.

That's a lot of holm-oak
(heavy, slow to combust). She's seventy-odd.
It keeps her young, she jokes.

The next time we go past,
cep-hunting in November, there's
no dog, no greeting, just

a sheer cliff of logs in the shed
and a few scattered on the grass.
She never used a wheelbarrow, I said.

Two years on and the stack's
still there, along with the dropped
ones, now furred with moss, and black.

Millennia ago they'd have made
a pyre against the greater cold
or carried the lot to her tomb's shade

for time to consume.
Sufficient for the life after.
Or enough to resume:

this was the pith
of her, always ahead of the first
frost. This was her faith.

POWER

The worst done for the best reasons,
and vice-versa: they'll stick out

a mile, bigger than your standard pylon,
the north coast's sea-swell

wired to Edinburgh's glare
down glen after glen, looping over braes.

It's an ailment, someone said,
in a different context: this need

for power. *A necessary
shot in the arm*, says Scottish Cabinet:

yes, like the silken skin of that girl
punctured by needles to the wrist,

catching her blood on a terry towel.

SPRING CLASS

My students gaze soporifically as I fillet Plath,
intent on enthusing – like a star chef courting
the suspicion that an inch below the froth
he can barely fry an egg: *un ignare*, a fraud.

The cobbled court of the old Vauban fort
turns southerly with sunlight, enough to permeate
a long skirt. Inside it's that winter in Fitzroy Road,
her avalanche of poems through inadequate heating

and the long freeze of '63 that I
recall as a bout of sledging . . . being old enough,
at six. I see their fingers subliminally
summing my age, drawn by this MacGuffin;

their mouths now open in surprise – much more
than when I lift the lid on her suicide
(the kids asleep, the milks, the new au-pair).
Or that is my impression. And what's really hiding

behind the steam of words is a lost reference
to my brother and I as we squeal down the track's
schillerised slope . . . to swerve into the fence,
snapping a runner, the snow sharp as axes

under its feathery asbestos fluff: look,
it's spotting with the excitement of my cut chin, my red
smudge of courage. Amazing, after the earthquake
of it all, to find I am here in class, instead.

ELSEWHERE

Käsmu, Estonia

The thunderous jet-sigh of coastal pines,
the midnight length of wolves, grandmothers
buried the far side of those massive boulders
geologists term 'erratic', brought there
as they were by a grinding of ice, left behind
like pebbles: here, I feel strangely at home –

right from the first time, when I came with the others.
And rather than settling in your northern folds,
the author of erratic, long-vowelled lines,
learning your secretive language to clear my mind,
tramping your woods, I'll keep you as an elsewhere:
sidled up to now and again; always torn from.

DISASTER

We carried out an impact assessment
on their people's grief;
flexed its brittleness,
broke it. Their sorrows were sorted,
its underlying causes mapped, made
respondent to emergent needs.

Tears were seen to leave lines
on their dusty faces
by our front-line team; we were not there
to invent the wheel, but to work
in collaboration with the necessary forces
for change, then move
the change forwards to another peg.

Carts rumbled over ruts
as we embedded behaviours,
made results tangible in the crowds
running like a wash of water in front of our bonnets.
The occasional spill led to a change
strategy, that sustainable and measurable solution
already described. When the phones went
it was only the phones – feedback
leaving its legacy, an effective
listening through the swarms of flies.

The magnitude of it all was a challenge
to our proven methodologies: they wept
when we left – buzzed and energised
by driving that evolution
for so many days, so many nights,
glad of home and of our own cries.

NIAGARA

1

It was not the infinite kilowattage
in the falling of the falls themselves

that most impressed, but the bouncing
top edge watched from the railed-off side:

that strange green water-dance
ledged against the sky, all that river-enthusiasm

colliding on the surprise of a vista of air —
as if God was suddenly to come across

His own absence, or that human trick
He's never quite fathomed

called letting your hair down,
called letting everything go.

2

That industrial, uroboric roar
drowned our lines as we shouted in macs

behind a door of water in the rock,
preferring the litotes of *not bad, hey?*

to open amazement. The tunnels
hacked out of the cliff, puddled,

were like Dante's Malebolge . . . while a single rock-fern
nodded outside on a slicked ledge, its garden-green

warded by the unbarrelling itself
from whatever lies beyond perpetual storm.

JÄÄÄÄR

That, in Estonian, it means 'the edge of ice'
seems hardly a surprise:
the melting away of consonants,
the freezing of vowels into a howl. Once

the entire bay would be tundra from November;
now it's slush, and snow something to remember.
I see that final *r* retreat to the 'yuh' sound
with less and less of that ice-bound

middle part I am incapable of pronouncing right
(the skater toppling, the fledgling's first flight
too soon after winter), as if the Baltic's lapping higher
till all that's left's a last, fish-hook cry.

BADGER

Each night at the same time his shadow
crosses over below Verdeilles, glimpsed white
like a stripe of snow on a black bough:
lumbering unworried, with a vicious bite.

It's the road that crosses the badger, you say —
his ancestry deep, the behaviour tied
to custom; the ancient setts concealed from the day,
each night's an echo of the previous night

where we are the ones who interfere:
he just stands his ground. Were a car to appear,
all death and dazzle, he wouldn't swerve, or wait:
his commitment's grown in his blood, like fate.

Where his front paws go his back ones follow
in a visa's double stamp, those claws' high fives.
Droppings glisten in the small hollows
he digs here and there, so long from our lives.

He'd despise (if he could) the parasitic dogs
who behave as if we matter; or the surrendering rabbit;
or the others that use us, like the cat, the fox.
But only we can despise — out of long habit.

MYTHOS

In memory of Fred and Judy Busch

'*I hear mythos padding in the underbrush*'

The brownstones still prop the wrought-iron gate
on Morton Street, *44A*
no doubt the same old porcelain plaque
you'd pass with Judy

in those early Greenwich Village days
to reach your one-room, wooden,
eighty-four-dollars-a-month flat
back in '63; you writing nights

on the edge of the bath, typewriter
poised on the toilet seat, icy air
and endless 'heartbreak in the mails'.
And now you're both passed away –

so abruptly gone I can't help thinking
of that note you slipped
under my hotel door in Deauville
after we'd planned to drive to Omaha

Beach: *The trip is too long. Fred.*
It seems like only yesterday, of course,
that the machinery of friendship was oiled
and running – that we cared how

the other was and what they were doing
and where the goddamn books were going to
('The third Armagnac ought
to get it out of you . . .'), with our lives

outflung behind us and before. I ought
to have been visiting your house in Maine
but for toxic luck's voracity; instead,
my little pilgrimage has ended

in this: a New York roar of indifference
beyond the disbelief. You cherished
one another more than any couple
I have ever known; would

have smiled to see me here . . . just like
your novel, stopped mid-stream.
Still struggling to imagine the rest, no
second thoughts and the keys stuck.

Nature's judged it nicely
with that girl on the bench, who's spoilt it all
with a wahoo *copain*
and a languid swell of bubble-gum
developing at her mouth like a medical illustration
as she consults her iPhone.

Before her, where the park's
small lake eructates the *source* even in drought,
they found a Roman capital
covered in vulva, like cleft peaches.
No, more labial than peaches;
though fashioned from marble

with a crude chisel, they convey
the thing itself, shaven
as close as a classical underarm
and repeated all round, over and over.
It's not on display, for the sake I suppose
of school groups, though a teacher could imply

it was fruit, a tree's-worth of apricots
or figs fissuring after a summer squall.
Now in the depths of the pittosporum
there are trysts that serve a variety of tastes;
while the stone statues of the *ancien régime*
reprieved by limewash and gazing

out from their locked-in time
of gods and nymphs and scanty chemises
look harmless enough, standing about like men
too old to be wrong. I find some grass at last
that's clear of dogs' laxation or broken glass
and read about the Revolution; how afraid

foppish Robespierre was of others' flesh.

WRITER

Nervily perfectionist, he cracks
syllables and removes words

as once he reduced daddy-long-legs
to their vernacular of trunk

as a secret favour to his grandmother,
who had to flap her hands

otherwise, reading in the deckchair
on the summer lawn. Did she wonder,

perhaps, why at eight years old
her grandson was still crawling around

with his nose so close to the ground
on such a gorgeous day?

HOLBEIN

Tate Britain

'Once I was alone with a Leonardo . . .'
The crowd thickens, stands in rows
three-deep, as if waiting for a train.

This is great art's business end:
the traffic of eyes in our passing glances
makes meaning manifest

in what, you agree, would otherwise
stay merely unique – straddling lifetimes
with the ease of the chosen, set

behind glass like a saint's relic.
Though there's something flirtatious
about these slow-moving rooms, hushed

like a church, where certain faces
become almost familiar and unlike the art
will pass out of our lives for good:

that willowy girl with slight vitiligo,
the loud hipster with his lateral thoughts.
And good's the word; here war

is an anomaly, greed perverse:
the invisible brushwork is its own heaven.
The young appraise and cannot imagine

the world existing without themselves in it;
while the old know, under their county
shocks of white hair, that it will (without them)

do quite well. They've got off lightly, after all,
to be stood here still, squeaking the floorboards
on their well-to-do heels, vituperative

or cast in wonder while there's time to be so.

UNDERGROUND

In the crypt of St Gilles du Gard
my wife sings, with a dozen others,
la Messe de Nostre Dame by Guillaume de Machaut.

It is damp and cold; a candle ungathers
its flame in a draught. The murdered papal legate
is laid along the cloister, under a pockmarked

slab, where even in drought
there is always water. Bad stuff
starts from a single point in time.

Near the well where, in 1562,
the priest and his choir boys were dropped
through its webs, Gilles the hermit's tomb

lies rough and thick, as if shaped by a mallet.
To touch it, the pilgrims would come in vast
numbers, all sweat and clamour, scattering

the mast and straw of nights on the road.
Was it all in vain? Nothing improved,
the age not turning over a new leaf,

death still setting its milestones
of war and plague. The *Front National*
runs this town and her peeling, piss-smelling

streets are sinister. Now the *Kyrie*
rises in overlapping petals of full-voiced tones
to break and shower us from the vaulted ceiling

or dim into the distance of tombs and stone –
the beauty and the bleakness so beguiling together,
like faith; like the government of faith by grief.

SECOND HOMERS

No, not Jones's 'weathered mantle-rock'
but the tussocked drystone of a terrace wall,
unbrowbeaten by frost, mossed through centuries,
toffee-hammered in minutes as I watched

the backhoe digger at work next door.
The past's luggage lost, the new destination
an intestinal circuit-board of pipes and wires:
the rough surgery of the Normans' pool.

Out with the chick-peas, onions, leaks,
the few rows of vines for the style.
Three weeks of sunburnt mirth a year
just where each spring we'd hear the nightingale.

VIA

As in a dewy meadow lit by dawn
at least the conquered could see

(in cobbled mortar or beaten earth)
the threads by which Rome spun control

and held her sway: the stout bridges tackling
the floods' shout on sharpened piers;

the milestones' clipped precision; or the inns
of fare where grooms rubbed down the frothed

horses, still shivering from the effort
it took to measure even the Empire's thumb.

It was clear, the oppression; its dust
settling on your tongue: that heft, that strength.

Those wheels, those hooves, those feet. There was no secret
to it. The central point was a pillar of stone

in the Roman forum – about which everything
revolved and back to which everything

came as the suspended ball in a game
of skittles rests from its swing: a needle of stone,

a node, something to kick at, not the end of the road
but the beginning, the start, the journey controlled

as a finger alters the flight of a kite on its long,
invisible string, twitched from afar to be turned.

Mounted, with baggage and arms, an officer
could make ten miles by dusk; a Brit, to get

to Rome, would need a good six weeks
of a nerve steadier than murrain, bandits, mud.

Distance was understood: and how it controlled.
Now what keeps us checked is far less clear.

All roads lead to Riyadh, yes, but the ways
are of air and you will never walk them,

they won't climb the slope in hairpin swags
or vanish into the arch of a gate. Only

the powerful use them, their wallets full of wars –
undertakers pacing before the coffined future

they have, with such infinite fuss, prepared.

INTERIOR WITH A YOUNG
MAN READING

after the painting by Vilhelm Hammershøi, 1898

Only pretending to be alone, of course,
leaning wanly in the unseen window's
northern light: knuckles as shiny as his black shoes

or the ebony wedge of desk ensnared
by the chair's back, its creamy fan of bars
as thin as his fingers against the dark book

whose words will not come right. His mouth's
got its draw-string concentrated look,
as if there's nobody here to impress.

It is bright out: the broad pine boards either tick
with heat or are chilled under snow-light
(the season remains unclear). And Vilhelm, of course –

insisting the shoes be polished over and over,
the scrubbed hands be helped with lanoline
to useful highlights – now keeps muttering,

through the slap of brushwork, 'No posing, no posing!
You are quite alone!' His brother's the genius;
he will be forgotten. Will the book's

thin wings take flight? Will the paint
be wet forever, the unknown life
always ahead of him and perhaps shorter

than the oyster light might lead one to expect?
Only the clock's quarterly clearing of its throat
reminds him, from time to time, to ask permission;

to flex his limbs from cramp and take a step.

ALCALÁ

11/3/2004: in memoriam

The guide book unread, it was a shock –
opening the hotel's curtains
with their snared litmus of smoke

to a dazzling installation of storks'
whitenesses, the wings half-snuffed to black
and spread in supernumerary arches

among the belfry's own, or gliding
low over the shocks of nest
that history's stony strictures had left alone.

Then the bombs flashed some four years
further down the line. Odd, how the bells'
tolling felt already as familiar

as the incumbent storks that
'always come back', you said.
As if returning was a wonder.

VESSEL

Saaremaa, Estonia

This rowboat's taken root and bloomed
its crew: a clinker-sided, wild-flower trough
in stonewashed blue by the corrugated shed

on an island whose vowels are the way
this inlet's waters arrive through the plumed
reeds – in a flat calm, lighter than the sky's grey,

on whiffs of bog-tar. The flowers are mostly red,
with a clutch of yellow comfrey bowed
over the sky-washed oar-bench. Was this designed,

so perfect in its fashion (that immaculate curve
of the gunwale up to the prow), the wreck allowed
its resurrection? Or has it simply remained,

untended, the rest down to the same verve
we've fought to master as if it had a mind:
the rotting hull a compost, and steerage feigned.

SUMMING UP

Each week he comes to the Home and entertains
the more 'able' residents (on voice and guitar)
in the so-called communal room at the far
end of the corridor, so the popular strains

of love's classics ('This being St Valentine's,'
the nurse laughs, hooking back the door
I'd firmly closed) now add the proverbial straw
to the pyre of loss. As your life grinds

to a halt (but not yet, not quite), *You Are*
the Sunshine of My Life crackles to a start.
He has a portable amp and a bigger heart,
does it all for free. I was hoping for

some last-words summing-up, a clap of thunder,
not songs that beat my finger against your palm:
the choric sorrows usurped by Andy's charm,
the cygnet's lament transfigured to Stevie Wonder.

CLEARING YOUR STUDY

1

Private realm of accounts, typed letters;
a book of unused Green Shield stamps;

meticulous inventories of minor expense;
bills and photos I pause under the lamp

to study, though (like a thief) I am short of time.
I am only doing this at your behest, of course –

the house must be cleared before it's sold –
but as I keep vigil in the nursing home

I feel I'm untying what keeps you fettered
or dismantling something that has grown too old,

foraging backwards as you weaken, get worse,
to the earliest generation of your Pan Am pens.

2

Or finishing you, perhaps. In the sleepless nights
I hold your hand and wish to be forgiven,

your breathing the moan of wind in sedge,
coming and going. (The Home murmurs

as nocturnal woods do, bustling with rumours.)
The muddle kept at bay, avoiding the edge,

your entire life has been tightly guyed
by the kind of order I envy, driven

as I am by the wisps of marsh-lights –
the filial verse you always read, loyal

to the end. Is this some obscure revenge –
working through your filing system, your desk

and cabinets, in some ultimate anarchist binge,
filling the bin-bags with paper in a clownish burlesque?

3

Any time now, they say. You've no idea
what I'm doing, though I've whispered it to you

between pointing out the pheasant by the wood
through your room's plate-glassed view –

the opening to your after-life, I think, in a russet
English perfection . . . though to step outside

is to find Basingstoke down in the valley, to hear
the laboured moan of traffic, and my anthropic dread

descends as the tyres scrunch the gravel
and I head back to attack the rest, unravelling

the years, the decades. I'm forced to bust
the lock on your old briefcase, like parenticide,

4

with a hammered spanner. It has to be done,
or others will do it and I'll never see again

your lifetime's grace, the honey in its cells.
I pillage, make flash decisions on what to keep

(gardening catalogues and suchlike ephemeral data)
or chuck (once-vital statements from banks), then sleep

in a welter of paper. Even the junk mail's
prized: a health-insurance offer with *Think About*

This scribbled on the top; ten years later
I wonder if you did. Your bouts of gout

aside, you were mostly fit until my mother died.
Then the grief dragged like weights and you began to slide.

5

I reach into the bowels of your oldest files:
what are lives but the illusion that all this

matters? So easily scattered, it slides
into the third bin-bag, already obese,

in a landslip of receipts (mostly shillings)
from long-dead stores, more recently-accumulated miles

never used, the special offers milling
with ancient reminders marked, in biro, *Replied*

to. I feel like stopping, but continue like a hacker
drunk on power. It has to be done! As a boy

I revered this realm, tiptoeing in from my toy
universe to gaze in wonder at what I now attack

with barbarian ease, as though it's the only
way to release you from an empire of pain.

Back in the Home, it's the early hours again,
and nothing bothers you but the fight to breathe.

Your study is almost done. There's something lonely
about you, now: I've stacked the pictures, I've stripped

the drawers to the proverbial final paper clip
and now you're on your own, the warmth of my palm

a faint clue, perhaps, to what you were. Bequeathed
only by my beseeching, your page-and-a-half of memoir

is still in the typewriter, stopped at the war,
curled like a buried scroll in its strange calm.

EXTREME UNCTION

I ask for the priest and an hour later
the local vicar bounds in,
tracksuit-togged, no dog-collar.

I mumble something about extreme
unction: prayers, oils. 'That's not
our thing,' he chuckles. 'Now,

what would you like me to do?'
I confess my father had served in church –
that he was a man of faith, that faith

had helped him cope with loss –
while the man in trainers briskly nods.
He leans his tall frame over the bed

beside the cotton swabs, the cold tea,
the untouched biscuits on the plate,
and booms out undeterminedly, finishes off

with a concession to ritual in the Lord's Prayer,
intoned as if it's old hat, a plough horse,
too holy for his gleamingly blunt world.

A pained expression creeps over
my unconscious father's face –
exactly as it did when, sharpening

the carver over the Sunday roast's
tucked-in tibial succulence,
head cocked as if listening out

for something like a reed-pipe, way off,
he'd test the blade with his thumb . . .
still not happy. Or not quite: not yet.

UNFINISHED

Your memoirs end, as on a little frown:
And then there was the war.
One-and-a-half pages of yellow feint-
ruled foolscap, curled in the typewriter
from the day your bed was moved downstairs.

'I can't get up to the study,' you'd maintain
to my periodic urging, the fighter
in you winged. Or: 'Too much of a chore.
Anyway, I can't imagine anyone
could possibly be interested in my affairs!'

Well, I was. So I carried the machine down
to where all your life lay now, set up a space
among the medicines on the table . . .
and it made no difference. I offered
to record you, but you shook your head,

claiming tiredness: 'I am incapable.'
Now I grope for what you said, over
the years, not even sure of which RAF base
it was in Lincolnshire so many were blown
from your life: at twenty you saw the dead

grow from friends in the nighttime canteen's calm:
the one who'd always feared Berlin, until
the Berlin sortie came and you know the rest;
or the chaps limping in from a dicey op
who flamed up before your gaze, trying to land.

I've plenty of this, and I do my best,
now you're gone; but beyond the hedge-hopped
fields and the skimmed wires I see metal,
burning: and no one's stepping out, unharmed,
with a filled pad of foolscap in his hand.

REMEMBERING MY FATHER

Pan Am, 1947–79

New York for you was always the boss:
home of the daft telex, the cross-
eyed command filtering through

to hassles on the tarmac, those delays in fog.
You'd nip over for a day, too brief for jet lag,
complain how the baggage-handlers at JFK

were infiltrated, were in the Mafia's pocket.
Only later would I learn not to take it
all as gospel, in the same way

you'd smile knowingly at 'The World's
Most Experienced Airline', or the centrefold
daring of that 'Clipper' calendar for '72

I hung in my bedroom, where I lusted
most of all for topless August
like a pilot choosing from his crew.

And now our taxi-driver, a retired
Midtown doorman recovering from (or fired
because of) a stroke and 'too much booze',

tells us how it's 'all the Mob, the food here . . .'
pointing out each curbside pizzeria
as we hurtle down the Boulevard through

Howard Beach – which, yes, sits right next
to the sprawling empire of jets
whose perpetual departures mimic the white egret

and creamy ibis we've watched each day
from our rented house in Jamaica Bay . . .
and I miss you again in a hush-kitted roar of regret.

FULL MOON IN SUMMER

Sight the moon through your fixed fist
and she'll slip away,

if slower than a fish —
like the monthly list

of things to do,
too long to be done.

And she's certainly
all glare tonight, gusted

into strobe-light by trees.
Our bedroom swarms

with her white sound,
the stars are dazed from sight.

We close our shutters but
she creeps around, ablaze with vacancy,

not letting us sleep. The night
sky's cloudless, and she can't

go shadowing her own face
from the light; but thinking

how months flash like cards
I reckon she might as well linger

on my life's flicker
with her motionless scree

of impact scars: a hypothetic,
destinal sun.

TELLING YOU ABOUT KRIBI

You like the photo of me, long-haired and gauche,
reading Ted Hughes in my swimming trunks on the rocks
in Cameroon, the mangrove beyond the clean black
sands a grey blur, the odd fisherman's pirogue
like a dropped leaf, my throne's volcanic stack
pocked where the lava once bubbled to the ocean

that seemed to sneak its way past Fernando Po
to find this lovely bay and expressly bury
its breakers in a gentle swell at my feet, their strung
glory under a crown of spume long spent. The very
idea of it, back then: of not being young!
My bare back says it all: nothing goes slower

than life when warm air's measuring your spine
and most of the stage is in front (if chance should smile).
I tell you that Exxon's got its tankers there now –
the arse end of six hundred and fifty miles
(the nodding pumpjacks among Chad's bony cows)
of forest-slicing pipeline, ruthless to the final

drop. The sacred grounds are a reek of garage,
farms interloped by oil, fish dead in the sea . . .
The promised schools and clinics were the usual fibs:
the money's also leaked. We lack the agility
of the spirits; we should be dancing there in Kribi –
hammering on calabashes, masked, in a trance of rage.

THE GIFT

for Anastasia

Like Paddington, this little bear
propped on the old beam up to your
now mostly empty bedroom, has a pedigree,

remember? We were all playing
'Give Us a Wave' in the dunes of Sweden
(the bright clapboard houses so straight-laced

among the birch and aspen), when a gull,
circling overhead, dropped the catch
it had plucked from the waves: fur-naked

(bar a scarf of ribbon) and waxlike
from salt, its tiny surprise still filled
your hand, back then, when you were five.

POSY

in memoriam A-C

We buy the flowers together, my daughter and I.
'Who are they for, mademoiselle?'
For a girl killed at dawn on Armistice Day,

leaving a club with a drunk at the wheel.
Magnesium-bright, *ensoleillée*
in her white wellingtons, the future

was hers, breath after breath to that infinitude
an eighteen-year-old assumes is her right.
The Mini Cooper demolished a wall.

My daughter bears the posy home
by the same route they'd walk from school,
the two of them: *Anne-Charlotte,*

she's written on the tag, after the printed
MADEMOISELLE. She says, once home, how weird
it was; the flowers grew heavier and heavier, until

'I felt I was carrying her, instead.'

FLAUBERT'S DRAFTS

Second thoughts, third thoughts, fourth thoughts,
the underbrush of lost causes, the barred ideas,
the hanging-about in the margins, the rejects

that never found their place, areas like frowns
or ploughed-up fieldwork on slants
where only the in-between scraps survived:

if only our lives offered such remedies –
the aching climb to the summit of perfection
able to go back upon itself, keeping the peak

in view, the nibbled vane of the quill
swerving and dipping over its own landscape
that alters according to the climber's will.

Instead we're left with regret, solid as hewn
wood, and the well-intentioned cleft we tread
from the blank plain: our one, uncorrectable line.

NEIGHBOUR

i.m. Claude M.

You have to tiptoe over a slope
of terracotta tiles; act the ballerina.
A dead weight when he fell,
and no EU-ordered rope,

only that broken marker-string
(on what is termed the 'verge'),
he caught his foot in. No one,
of course, heard a thing.

Discovered in the foetal position
like a warrior in his stone-lined cist,
the only grave goods were the brick
walls beside him, all but finished: his mission

before retirement, with room for his dad.
That long dream of living there
he'd described to me once (stood together
on the brute concrete foundation pad)

as *more precious than gold. A kind of birth.*
Now it's all done – wired, painted –
it's hired to the hunters, who feast and laugh.
Hard to know what a house is worth.

DRY STONE WALLING

You know that sudden need: to repair, to make
amends. Restoration where the hard white sky
has bitten chunks out, where a lone sag of barbed wire
serves as sentinel – its miniature scalps taken

off would-be escapees. You watch your fingers
like hawks, for stones can roll: a knuckle no match
for their unaccustomed weight, that strange mineral flash
of life, the will that spars with your wedding ring

through the heavy glove: granite, leather, gold.
Your knees in mud. This time for definite, for good,
solid from the bottom, stayed by a heaviness of head
and poise. Though nothing stays where you want it, soldered

only by calculation; its sheer weight.
Wobble and tilt – those bids for freedom. The weather
runs at everything: you're trying again where your father
clicked and clacked like a clock all the way to the gate.

SUBTRACTION

Cap Bon, Tunisia, 2003

El Haouaria, where they hollowed out
Carthage, is now a vaulted omega of absence,
its caves striated by slaves whose daylight bout
was a dim, powder-fashioned shaft,
who lived, breathed and doubtless died sandstone,
its colossal blocks floated up the coast on rafts

to count as bits of Punic monuments
that were swept away by a Roman broom
(by order of the Senate), with salt spread
for good measure, so not even scrog could bloom.
Beneath the silence you can hear the moans.
To think this might have been us, instead

of our own life's latitude! El Haouaria,
a honeycomb of vowels we get wrong
like most visitors (preferring 'that quarry
on Cap Bon'), is where it all belongs:
the temples, the arenas, the entire city.
Like Lego, it will not go back into the box,

but here is its negative: each axe-chip fits
its equivalent bump, the subterranean dark locks
onto its reverse, heliotropic and built
high – the Manhattan of its day. One moment it's there:
the next it's gone. *Like us*, I whisper . . . it being unfair
to say this in front of the kids, who're yet to be filled.

IN YORK MINSTER

*The glass in York Minster is 90% naturally coloured,
without added colourants.*

Tempered to this miracle from forest ash
('and yet nys glas nat lyk asshen of fern'),
they must have cleared whole coombs
and cols of their bracken, its stubborn
rust scraped off for the fiery womb:
the quantity of potassium needed was vast.

Two hundred kilos of wood per one of glass!
For colourlessness, coppiced beech
on lime-rich soil; for green panes, beech on clay.
Between the leads they fused what we cannot reach
from entire forests, it seems, to field the play
of sunlight – as did the trees over their floors of mast.

THE SWIMMING POOL

Kinshasa, 1968

Our gardener would rake its gloom
like a patch of ground, stirring it

to a distressed, even darker core
of the almost-living and the nearly drowned:

scooped with a net for the rusty bucket,
he'd pour them out in the no-man's-land

before the proper bush: each night's haul
a sprawl of drunken guests, bristling

with feelers and sodden legs, still
in a rush to be free: capsized hulls with oars,

tiny nests of torment. Frogs swooped
between the slippery hair of the concrete sides

and the blind, sedimented depths
they'd jack-knife into. This was the door

out of the air's stickiness, the scratch of lawn:
our clumsy paradise. We'd swim with care

among the fresh spoil steeped at eye-level,
become huge and forlorn: thorax still beating

and beating on a simple heart; mouth-parts
searching for air like a man's last words;

a moth's hopeless wingspread. Where
could I start? I handed out names to faces;

buried the drowned like birds.

HALF CENTURY

The years are always something we think of
as vaguely surprising, guests that come and go
who might have been expected to hang around,

entertaining our disappointments, letting us forget.
We count them every so often like marks against us,
or a row of sacks bulging with what we can't

yet throw away and wonder (after a certain age)
how we'll ever manage without them.
The truth is, they don't stay. Fifty

seems too much, you say, but remember
they have gone: what's left is not to be weighed
but savoured, like love. We want

to keep them back for some unfocussed good,
one minute worrying about being too young,
guessing what the rules, invented

in our absence, demand of us; and then we see
that all along the game was being cooked up
at every instant to give us that impression

when really no one's in charge and there's nothing
but a vague skein like silk or torchlight
connecting this to that – the present spiced only because

the past's no longer suffused, the future not yet
seasoned. So we'll drink to us, not to time's tribunal,
and braid each year with hugs like an old friend.

ON A PHOTO OF A
WAINWRIGHT'S SHOP

On the day of its sale, before being dismantled
and the site redeveloped: Hungerford, 1951

This was where they made
each thill of dung cart, or jackwain's tailboard;
where what turnips knocked from their sacks
got shaved, the bolts locking the top rave,
the summers joined to the shutlocks to hold hops;

or where the strouters first firmed the wagon's side
as the unmacadamed roads made of the nave
every labourer's shuddering fulcrum – until in for the kill
came the oiled pistons, the heedless Ford,
and all this was obliterated as so many facts

are in history, and one by one the wainwrights died
along with those they called the *liners*, who travelled
like the sawyers from shop to shop, their only canvas
the naked, chamfered wood of spoke and board,
turning that practical good into something

no one needed: Berkshire the yellow of a chanterelle,
Wiltshire a harebell's blue to the iron tyre.
Here is where the old world got upgraded
and our nescience unfolded, that day
the doors closed on the dark and the sign said SOLD.

REPRIEVE

Driving down from the Alps we were reassured:
a late, hard frost, its hoar taking its keen scalpel

to the forests; the birch bled to the last bud,
the spruce and firs flayed, twinkling yet scrupulous;

even on the lower slopes, starched to a pause,
the pines stood, formal and glazed as footmen.

Flick anything here and it would ping (I joked)
like crystal: thankfully normal, a sign that all

is on seasonal course in our broken weather glass;
that age can be reversed; that whoever's top

of the table has suddenly turned to the servant
and said: 'Send my man down to them. It's

time we had a miracle. More wine, Faust?'
And God never does facetious (or so that vicar said).

IN BED

I've heard it maintained that a roadless country lacks conviction,
like a life without a sense of direction, a plan.
But surely a single life can spread like a fan,
be an entire Mongolian plain, not a waste of dereliction?

Maybe that *is* a little confusing, given we travel
in one basic direction, from A to wherever we're led
to in the alphabet: which is always the sleep of Z.
Yet must we, like Holland, be mapped – or else unravel?

Sheep-tracks served on St Kilda. Winds would lock
them in for weeks. No roads, no wars. The land
in perfect fusion; for roads mean right hand, left hand,
verge and division. The island's only way was rock

and grass, every edge of it opening onto ocean.
Let us say it was like your body, over which
my fingers are free to wander (an invisible stitch
of desire): a country where nowhere is a deviation.

PANIC

Hitting *Cuisines* in the new IKEA,
besieged by hobs, I was paralysed

by the arrows on the floor.
This is the only way, they claimed,

through the rooms' pretence
where couples were dimpling beds

with practice bottoms, yanking
at fairy-lights, stocking up on

what my mother would call,
as far as I remember, 'sundries'.

I started to walk against them,
counter to the flow, knowing

those shelves only had books as a sop
to types like me who don't

exist in the real world: solecistic
in the perfect grammar of hob and bed.

Incorrigible, I emerged in daylight
as someone might who, escaping

from a theatre's fug mid–scene,
finds himself out on stage,

dazzled; pretending to be gratified
by his own applause.

CHECKING BLOOD PRESSURE

It's the same old trick: making you think,
as the cuff goes on, that each puff up
to the squeeze and squeeze and squeeze

is a tender thing: the reassurance
of the bloated god with time
on his hands, a helpful hand on the arm,

a kind teacher's touch:
not the blood cut off, the clasp
that's overdone, or the relief when,

sighing in that same old rubbery way,
he is gone for another year, and it's all
retrenchment behind the bonhomie.

MARGINALIA

History breathes in silence,
watched from afar. Ordericus Vitalis,
'benumbed with winter frosts',
lays down his weary, twelfth-century pen

in his *Historia Ecclesiastica*
I'm reading in Dean Church's translation
from a Cambridge compilation of sources
dated (the soundless shell-bursts!)

1918. A long telescope
of scholarship, yet the bench
creaks as the old monk labours
over his letters in the cold.

The smews tuck in their wings
on the abbey's frozen lake
where grey lags, blurred from wind,
say *kark, kark*. Their arrows soon

to puncture all that laborious
prose as usual, heralds
to 'the soft air of spring'
and all that he would rather sing of

transfigured into leaf
before the gadfly heat
of summer, the wafts of dung,
the craving again for frosts.

IN COURT

The accused turns her head and our eyes meet:
two bore-holes face me, ringed by fatigue. *Le vide.*

Manipulatrice. I feint a smile; the family don't.
Always a terror, huge, built like a man. Even her son,

ashamed of his dad's loose ways with the girls,
says he regrets what she did. A gruelling

July heat over three days, the neighbours
noticing a smell. From under the stairs,

newly sealed with a sheet of plasterboard
and a lick of paint, something leaked. A body

is mostly water, the judge declares. Did you
not know that? Or really think your

husband would simply shrivel and dry
like a fig? She whispers, 'I did'. And the family

around me stir and smile (knowing her well),
while she stays put in her own leak-proof hell.

But you can see the logic in it, I think, as the witnesses
speak, sob, praise him like the lover he was,

no doubt, of several among them . . . the divorce
meant everything divided, from the little dream house

to the pool she'd dug, the neighbours said,
with her own bare hands. And what do you share with the
   dead,

who take nothing with them, and never return?
The logic of bare hands, that: or history's slow burn.

PUNCTURED

The taut membrane, nail-splittable,
of my brother's Fokker back in '64:

ready for the maiden after months of *until*, now
waiting for him to take the bus from school.

Stretched so taut, tappable, like a drum. Such
temptation. *All it would take* was my only thought,

like later leg-overs separated from me
by the last and impossible distance of lunge.

ROADS THEMSELVES ARE SILENT

The motorway's sough beyond the hill's beech
is not motors so much as tarmac and rubber,
a word like *indubitable* over and over,
failure only in the skid's squeal –

that tell-tale scar like a dark ladder.
And what if the urubu of wooden wheels,
the Xhosa clicks of hooves on cobbles,
the smack of the loose manhole cover

that keeps us awake, or the morse
after midnight of those lone high heels
might betray themselves to speech:
what would they say? That roads

themselves are silent; they make *us*
speak. Even the fervent pressure of pilgrims
on the bleak ways between dangerous wastes
leaves behind it – what? A silence.

Like that quiet of the museum
with its stretch of peat-pegged track,
dark from its bog and forlorn, as mute
as a rim-impression in Roman marble.

And what a frightening thought, that everything
is always on its way to somewhere else,
whatever route we pick – eternally
advancing to the promised goal

like armies whistling over the trapped
boots' drum, their standards flapping,
their knees as one. Though silence
is following them, as well.

VOLUNTARY

North Wootton Common, Norfolk

Pools are spreadeagled
and the near marsh
suggests itself oozily under the grass, but a flock
of geese straddles
the raised pass

on which I'm heading
for the one gate
in the long alder-mess of hedge: I
hesitate and then
walk on, watching

the birds levitate
en masse into a clear
blue winter sky on a broken-harmonium
medley of cries
to shape, if vaguely,

their conventional V
and head towards the delta
I cannot see. A few separate like rebellious
adolescents,
flecks I track

across the sky's screen
as if fretful for them,
until they wheel with a suitable insouciance
and join the group,
its wake already

dissolving in distance
(the flock's shadow
bounced by the grass, grey as ash, less
uniform and swifter as it sweeps
over me and screens

the sun in a flash).
All but one, that is – who's
doggedly travelling the other way, so completely alone
I could give it a name,
consider its fate.

I feel like shouting
out but can't.
Tough luck swerves for no one: probability's
the curve it pursues
until its dot

assumes its own
extinction . . . a voluntary
exile, free at last – or condemned to a lonely
end in some oil-slicked
pool, garbage tip

or waste of choppy sea
I can so easily
imagine as I carry on regardless to the rusty gate,
its top cross-bar
garlanded with barbed wire,

its latch a palliative I cannot take.

ACKNOWLEDGEMENTS

Acknowledgements are due to the editors of the following: *Times Literary Supplement*; *Poetry Review*; *ATOL − Art Therapy Online*; *Alhambra Poetry Calendar*; *Love Poet, Carpenter − Michael Longley at Seventy*.

'Via' and 'Roads Themselves Are Silent' were commissioned for broadcast by BBC Radio 3's *Between the Ears*.

I am deeply grateful to the Estonian Writers' Union for a grant towards the writing of this volume as well as generous accommodation at the Union House in Käsmu.

The brief quote in 'Second Homers' is from the last lines of 'Rite and Fore-time' in David Jones's *The Anathémata* (1952).